What's Your Why? is ideal for those looking to gain new perspective on how their inner motives, interests, and needs can be clarified and harnessed for optimal career and self development. Written in an accessible style, it is designed for the busy individual who wants to step off the treadmill for a few moments to gain an extra edge through insight without the obscure theories of shallow exhortations of the typical management or career book. Best of all, it is authored by Kent Burns, consistently one of the leading talent recruiters working internationally. Kent has placed hundreds of professionals into top positions with Global 2000 firms, and his vast experience is here distilled into practical concepts that will hold value for anyone seeking to advance in his or her career. Brief, fun, and relevant, "What's Your Why?" will work for you.

David Pfenninger, PhD Founder - Performance Assessment Network & BubbleUp, Ernst & Young 2005 Entrepreneur of the Year Winner in Technology, Great Lakes Region

"Kent is in this business because of people. He loves to help them change their lives. In addition to the clients and candidates that he brings together, this can be seen directly in our office by the number of top producers here that he has mentored. Kent has perspective, leadership, knowledge and passion for excellence which others want to be associated with."

Zack Troyer, MRINetwork

"Kent is a man of integrity and incredible business savvy. He has proven to be a great mentor and motivator with a constant willingness to teach and share his vast wealth of knowledge. He is simply the most respected man I know in the recruiting business."

Micah Di Sabato, MRINetwork

"I regard Kent as one of the best recruiters and businessmen in the recruiting industry. He listens intensely to the client's needs and responds with no-frills delivery. Additionally, Kent has amassed a wealth of knowledge to better the jobseeker experience. He keeps a keen eye on the ever-changing workforce and how emerging processes and Technologies can better recruitment strategies."

Josh Akers, Regional Vice President, Direct Employers Association

"I highly recommend Kent. He has been a tremendous search partner for us over the past six years. Kent consistently delivers high quality candidates and successful hires. He understands our culture and what it takes to be successful here. He goes above and beyond to meet our needs while being a true business partner. We view Kent as an extension of our staffing team."

Shelley Devore, Director, Fortune 200 Company

Kent has the courage to ask difficult questions to get to the root of the needs for all involved, that is a rare talent."

Tammi Ramsey, Entrepreneur

What's Your Why?

How a three-word question can change you, your company, and the lives of those you lead

by

Kent Burns
with Silouan

Bloomington, IN Milton Keynes, UK

authorHOUSE™

AuthorHouse™
1663 Liberty Drive, Suite 200
Bloomington, IN 47403
www.authorhouse.com
Phone: 1-800-839-8640

AuthorHouse™ UK Ltd.
500 Avebury Boulevard
Central Milton Keynes, MK9 2BE
www.authorhouse.co.uk
Phone: 08001974150

First published by AuthorHouse 7/20/2006

ISBN: 1-4259-3544-3 (sc)
ISBN: 1-4259-3543-5 (dj)

Printed in the United States of America
Bloomington, Indiana

This book is printed on acid-free paper.

Quantity orders and not-for-profit book rates available from kburns@better candidatesfaster.com

This book is dedicated to the memory of
David Oberting, friend and mentor.

This book is also dedicated to my dad, Carl Burns, who faithfully fanned
the flame inside me.

Acknowledgments

This book would not have happened without the encouragement of my friend, Silouan. Thanks for walking with me every step of the way on this, and for giving up all those Saturday mornings to meet with me on this project. You are truly one of a kind.

To my friends at the Monon Coffee Company in Broad Ripple, Indiana: Thanks for letting us meet there every Saturday and for all the hot tea, coffee, blueberry scones, and pumpkin bread.

Thanks also to: Tammi Ramsey, Kirk Abraham, and John Oblazney, for allowing me to be an active participant as The Why changes your lives;

Zack Troyer and Tom Thurlow, for your thoughtful insights and for "getting it";

David Pfenninger, for your encouragement, confidence and investment in me.

Marc Drizin, for advice, input, and information; and Kelli Deal, the best executive assistant ever.

To my business partners Bill, Garth, and Chad, thanks for working with me to help all our people accomplish their Why.

Finally, thanks to the ones who know me best and love me in spite of it…you keep me going:

Daniel and Terry, I am a better man because of you both. Thanks for walking beside me through life – 2 Cor 11:1, remember?

Emily, you're just not right.

Haley, Max, and Abby, thanks for being the best kids in the world. You bring me joy.

Mom, Andrea and Evan, you're the best. Thanks for supporting me no matter what.

Dad, you are my inspiration and always have been. I could not have gotten here without you.

And Patti – thanks for loving me, supporting me, and deciding to take the journey with me. I don't know where the road leads next, but I'm glad we're traveling together.

Table of Contents

Prologue:

WHY I wrote this book

After working fifteen years as an accountant, within sixty days, I made a life-changing decision to leave accounting and corporate America behind.

I left a six-figure salary and took a 100 percent commission recruiting job that guaranteed me ZERO income.

Within four years, I was the number one individual producer worldwide at the largest recruiting firm in the world.

I am now an owner of that business and lead one of the most successful finance/accounting recruiting practices in the country.

I was able to make this transition because of The Why.

HOW this book can help you

If you are a leader or manager who aspires to drive your organization to increasing levels of excellence, this book will show you how to understand, uncover, and unleash the power hidden inside those you lead.

If you are a leader or manager who feels trapped in your current business environment, this book will help you better understand the core factors that motivate you. Knowing your Why will enable you to pursue the path toward a more meaningful life.

If you are an entrepreneur who has made the leap to actively pursue your Why, this book will help you understand and embrace the Why of those who work in your business. It will allow you to lead them to places they have never been. Your people will, in turn, take your business to places it has never been.

Introduction

I had been an accountant my entire career and after fifteen years, I was successful and able to lead a very comfortable lifestyle. But in the summer of 1999, everything changed. I was working for a major public accounting firm — one of the proverbial "Big Four"— and I was in a tough situation. My friend, Larry (a highly regarded partner) and I were attempting to launch a new service offering within the firm. While it was an exciting opportunity, there were high expectations and considerable pressure to deliver revenue and profit to the bottom line.

The firm had made a sizeable investment, and was eagerly awaiting the return. I was traveling all over the country, on and off airplanes, staying in hotels, eating bad food, and missing my wife and children. Despite our collective efforts, after eighteen months, Larry and I weren't meeting our own expectations or those of the firm. I was exhausted both physically and mentally. My relationship with my wife and kids had changed. I wasn't part of the weekly routine anymore - when I was home, I was in the way.

June 10, 1999. Larry and I were in Minneapolis making a presentation to a Fortune 500 client. It went well, and I remember feeling reasonably good about it. Sitting at the airport awaiting our flight home, I noticed Larry camped out at a payphone near our gate (his cell was dead). This wasn't uncommon for him, as he got dozens of voicemails every day. He looked sad, but I didn't think too much of it. Our assigned seats were in different rows, so we didn't get to debrief on the way home, as was customary for us after a big presentation.

Once we landed, Larry and I said our goodbyes at the gate and he headed straight toward the phones. I began the long walk to the parking garage and immediately became lost in a fog of thoughts that is all too familiar to frequent travelers. In the garage and almost to my car, I heard Larry's voice echoing behind me.

"Hey, Burns!"

I turned around and saw him walking briskly toward me.

"We need to talk."

Winded, he caught up to me and said, "Kent, I want to tell you something." Ominously, he added, "But I've been ordered not to disclose this to you until tomorrow."

Larry knew he could trust me, he'd known me for fifteen years. He proceeded to tell me that he'd been instructed to ask for my resignation the next morning. After eighteen months, the project was deemed a failure. I had not met my sales goals and the company had spent an enormous sum of money building an infrastructure for this venture that wasn't being utilized. The bleeding had to be stopped. My choice was to resign with dignity or be fired.

My heart sunk and a feeling of failure welled up in my stomach. Now this "thing" was out there, and neither one of us knew what to do next. I was exhausted from the trip, and so was Larry. In spite of the situation, we both just wanted to go home. After an awkward silence, we agreed to meet at 7:00 the next morning.

The thirty-minute drive home from the airport was an interesting one. Tomorrow morning was going to come, and I was going to tender my resignation — assuming I didn't wake up and realize that this was all a dream. I felt many different emotions: a sense of failure, fear, anger, resentment, embarrassment, and even relief. All kinds of things went through my head. My wife had been at home with our kids for many years and I was the sole provider. This would come as a shock. How would she respond? Soon others would find out. What would my friends think? What would the neighbors think? What would my kids think? For a guy who felt like he was in charge most of the time, things had spun out of control in so many ways.

I got home and told my wife. She was surprised, disappointed, and apprehensive, but handled it fairly well. After we talked for a couple of hours, the only thing to do was go to bed and try to get some sleep.

The next morning was a rough one. I got to the office and Larry was already there; neither one of us was looking forward to this. To complicate matters, we were scheduled to begin two days of internal meetings and had flown in several employees from around the country. They would arrive from the hotel within the hour.

Larry and I agreed to the terms under which I would resign and when we concluded, he stood up, walked around his desk, and hugged me. Now there was only one thing left to do. Larry and I walked into a conference room full of people who worked for me. I broke the news, and said goodbye.

It was June 11, 1999. I was officially out of work, and I was at a crossroads.

I'd never been in this position before. In the game of life (and that's the way I viewed it), I had played reasonably well thus far. I had been spared a defeat of this magnitude. Looking back, the news I got from Larry was a symptom, but it wasn't the problem. I was the problem.

One of the good things about being unemployed is you suddenly have time on your hands, time to do all the things you convince yourself you can't do when you are busy working. I had no immediate job prospects, and I had time. Time to ask, "What in the heck am I going to do now?"

Thankfully, we had some money saved, and through prayer and the counsel of my wife and close friends, I realized I needed time to sort things out. How long, I didn't know. Part of me instinctively wanted to jump right back in the game — to show "them" — and part of me just wanted to disappear. I desperately needed a break from all the noise in my head. Our house had a screened porch that looked out over a wooded backyard. It was a quiet place, and I spent many waking hours over the next few weeks just sitting out there. Slowly, clarity came.

I made a conscious decision not to panic. I made a conscious decision to step out of my black-and-white world and spend some time in the gray. I made a conscious decision to trust my faith, rather than put a "Christian face" on the outside while trying to fix everything all by myself on the inside. I worked hard to practice patience, which doesn't come easily to me. What a journey it turned out to be. In retrospect, it was during this two month time of renewal that the whole concept of "The Why" was born.

After some brutal soul searching, I came to the conclusion that I wasn't a very good accountant, and I didn't like being one very much either. I was sick of traveling and I wanted to be home every night with my family, sleeping in my own bed. I was tired of being told what to do, where to do it, and how to do it. I was tired of my earning potential being determined by someone who didn't have a vested interest in maximizing it. Wow, I sure was tired.

I had all kinds of questions. Why are certain things important to me? Why do my actions betray my words so often? Why am I so driven? Why do

I get up and trade "hours for dollars"? Why, at thirty-eight years old, do I not have more "things" figured out? Why am I on this path, and is it actually leading somewhere I am interested in going? I had been making big sacrifices to achieve a success that I hadn't even defined. I was looking hard for answers, in lots of places…and as my business partner, Bill Ritchie, says, "Nine times out of ten, the answer is in the mirror." I had come face to face with myself and had to answer the question: "What is my Why"?

There have been several distinct times in my life that, without question, God intervened to get me "out of the ditch" and "back on the road." The summer of 1999 was one of those times. I needed help and God provided it. Here's the wisdom that He revealed *to* me, ***about*** me.

I am first and foremost committed to God and to pleasing Him.
WHY: I believe it is why I am on this Earth to begin with.

I am committed to my wife and children, and to be the best husband and father that I can possibly be.
WHY: They are the most precious gifts in this life that I have been entrusted with. Their care and well-being is my responsibility. I am called to protect them, lead them, care for them, and provide for them. If I screw that up, not much else is going to matter.

I want a career that allows me maximum autonomy and flexibility.
WHY: I don't want to miss school plays, ballgames, doctor's appointments, helping with homework, and tucking my kids into bed at night. I want to be able to set my own goals, and be able to do what is necessary to achieve them.

I want an environment that empowers me and allows me to make positive things happen that benefit both me and the organization.

I want a career that offers me unlimited earning potential and personal accountability for my success or failure.

WHY: I want two things to determine my worth: my abilities and the marketplace — not corporate budgets, insecure managers, or "economic conditions." I want to know that whether I succeed or fail, it is largely a result of my own efforts.

I should pursue a career in sales that leverages my past experience.

WHY: I was a salesman trapped in an accountant's body. My gifts and talents are in interacting with people. I love the sales process, from start to finish. Finance and accounting are too far removed from the front lines of business for me.

Living life is like building a wall.

WHY: Life is a building process, and like it or not, we are continually building. We build our character, our faith, our marriage, our family, our relationships with others, our career, and ultimately, our legacy. Each day represents one brick in that wall, and you only get to lay one brick each day. You can't lay tomorrow's brick today, nor can you reposition or replace yesterday's brick. It is what it is. My definition of peace is lying down at night satisfied with the brick you laid that day.

My wall looked like something you would see touring the remains of ancient Greece. I was ashamed of the bricks I had been laying. So what now? As Napoleon Hill said, "Action is the best measure of intelligence." The fact remained that I was unemployed with no job prospects, and I had a wife and two children who were counting on me. It was time to act.

I did all the things the professionals tell you to do when you are looking for a job. I made a lot of phone calls, had some job interviews, networked with friends and colleagues, and worked with some recruiting firms. My journey led me to two men who would change my life.

George Ceryak and David Oberting ran one of the most successful management recruiting franchises in the world, and it just happened to be in Indianapolis. I had neither heard of them nor was aware of their success. I saw their ad in the Yellow Pages, and contacted them hoping their company could help me find a job. I had no idea that the "job" I ultimately landed would be working for them.

I met with them and learned they had recently lost their only finance and accounting recruiter. I also found out that a career in recruiting tapped into several of my Whys: Unlimited income, flexibility, autonomy, no travel. It leveraged my finance background, success or failure rested with me, and this company offered a family friendly culture.

That was the good stuff. It was risky — 100 percent commission sales; a big risk for a former accountant. We had some money saved, but it wouldn't last long. The only way to reconcile this piece of the puzzle was to take a leap of faith. After several days of talking and praying, my wife and I agreed to give it everything we had for six months, then we would re-evaluate.

The first three months were tough, as I made little, if any, money during that time. I had some doubts, but slowly I began to achieve success. By the end of 2000 (my first full year), I had become my office's top producer. By 2003, I had become the top producing recruiter within Management Recruiters International, outperforming over 3,500 other professionals worldwide.

When George and Dave recently retired, I was privileged to be one of four individuals who bought the business from them. It all reminds me of one of my favorite Bible passages:

> *"God can do anything, you know – far more than you could ever imagine or request or guess in your wildest dreams!"*
>
> - Ephesians 3:20, *The Message*

Besides a lot of hard work and a generous outpouring of grace, I believe my understanding and use of The Why is the key to my success. My clients rely on my ability to recruit and deliver not only the **best** person for their organization, but the **right** person for their organization. To do that well, I must understand and tap into their core motivating factors; that's where The Why comes in. Matching candidates with companies in such a fundamental way allows me to impact employee performance, employee retention, the value of a company's human capital, and the financial success of the organization.

All this has further convinced me what a powerful factor The Why really is. With the aid of my colleague, Silouan, I began to write about The Why. The result is this book.

Through my time of reflection and trial, I learned "What my Why" is. It changed my life beyond anything that I ever imagined. The emotions I felt are not uncommon — yet few people have their Why acknowledged, understood, or cared for. The Why has allowed me to enrich careers and impact lives. Utilizing the principles in this book, you will be able to understand and experience the life-changing power of The Why for you, your company, and those you lead.

Part 1
Understanding The Why

Section 1:
Where Is Your Treasure?

There comes a time in every rightly constructed boy's life when he has a raging desire to go somewhere and dig for hidden treasure.

- Henry A. Kissinger, former secretary of state

For where your treasure is, there your heart will be also.

- Matthew 6:21 NIV Bible

Robinson Crusoe Island is one of a tiny group of islands in the Juan Fernandez archipelago, approximately 400 miles off the coast of Chile. The island was once home to Scottish sailor Alexander Selkirk, the adventurer immortalized by Daniel Defoe as Robinson Crusoe.

Pirates and fortune hunters have long scoured the island in search of treasure that was stolen and buried there after the Spanish conquest of Peru in the sixteenth and seventeenth centuries. In 1715, a ship en route to Spain carrying the treasure landed there and the treasure was buried by a Spanish sailor. For nearly 300 years, people searched, including American millionaire Bernard Kaiser, who invested over $1 million in the hunt.

On September 27, 2005, the *Santiago Times* reported that a group of adventurers had discovered 800 metric tons of gold, silver, and jewels buried approximately fifty feet below the surface of the tiny island. Estimated value: $10 billion.

Consider the zeal with which those in search of buried treasure pursue their prize. Some devote their whole lives to little else. It dominates their thinking, planning, and actions. You may not be a treasure hunter in the literal sense, but we all have our treasures — things we value highly and go to great lengths to acquire, honor, or serve. When you think about it, few things in our lives truly qualify.

So where is your treasure?

If life has ceased to be fulfilling for you, if you look at those you lead and see apathy, I suggest a treasure hunt. If you've never been on one, perhaps now is your time. When people believe their effort will result in "treasure," the hunt is more intense, the reward greater.

Often the hunt for treasure is associated with fantasy, a waste of time, a dream that doesn't really exist. Ah, but it *does* exist. Deep inside all of us is treasure that isn't a dream. ***It is real, it is powerful, it is worth searching for, and it can be <u>found</u>.*** This ***treasure principle*** is one of the keys to understanding The Why and will maximize your energy and that of your people.

My co-author, Silouan, took a trip deep inside himself to find his treasure. Silouan was twenty-five, and to the world, appeared like he had it all. He was a tall, good-looking marine officer in fighter pilot training. He'd met his bikini-perfect wife on a Florida beach and his future seemed unlimited. However, Silouan's real treasure was buried, and this "Top Gun" façade was an image he actually had grown to hate.

Silouan had been a creative youth; a very spiritual boy who dreamed of writing books and poetry. But somewhere along the way, he got off track and over time, became what people thought he should be: the All-American hero married to a pretty blonde. In reality, his marriage was a failure and the military stifled his creative spirit and left him feeling empty inside.

On August 23, 1994, his world collapsed. During a training accident, his jet caught on fire and he had to eject. Only twenty feet above ground when the rocket seat exploded, Silouan broke his back, and his co-pilot died in the crash. Shortly thereafter, his wife left him and he descended into the depths of post traumatic stress disorder.

After a year of therapy, Silouan was released with a disability discharge. Everything for which he had trained over the previous six years was gone. All remnants of his false Why were gone. Staring at his future with no idea of what to do next, he knew he had to find a purpose.

He bought a motorcycle and decided to walk the earth. Traveling around the United States and Mexico, the freedom allowed his mind to open to his soul and rediscover the creative dreams of his youth. It was here, on the road, that he uncovered his treasure. His Why was creativity.

Since that day, he hasn't looked back. With no formal training, he has published an award-winning, internationally distributed magazine, *Bearfoot Journal of Northern California Outdoors*, become a singer, songwriter, author, successful entrepreneur, and is currently sharing what he learned about recovery by leading both incarcerated youth and adults through his "Learning to Fly" program.

Silouan found his Why. He found his treasure. You can find yours, too, and help others you lead find theirs. When you find it, your life (and theirs) will never be the same.

Do you know where your treasure is?

Section 2:

What's Your Why?

We must have a theme, a goal, a purpose in our lives. If you don't know where you're aiming, you don't have a goal. My goal is to live my life in such a way that when I die, someone can say, she cared.

— *Mary Kay Ash, founder of Mary Kay Cosmetics*

During a meeting a few years ago, I posed a question to the entire staff at my company. The question was simple. I asked them "What's Your Why?" Many in the group returned blank stares. Some nodded thoughtfully. Others smiled.

I continued, "Each of you get up every weekday morning, come here and work eight, nine, ten hours a day. Some of you come in on weekends… why?" Slowly, my audience came to life. I heard things like: "family," "security," "so my kids can go to a good school," "to make money," "to get out of debt," or "to prove that I can be successful." The answers were as unique and varied as the individuals in the room. Everyone has a reason for doing what they do. Not everyone is consciously aware of that reason. But it's there.

From that meeting forward, I have challenged the people at my company to answer the question "What's Your Why?" Many of them have discovered the value, both tangible and intangible, of embarking on that journey. It's a simple, yet daunting task, requiring introspection and honesty. Some find the initial answer to this question isn't the *real* answer to this question. The Why has layers, and we must dig until we get to the core. It often appears in disguise, but once unmasked, it reveals itself as a very personal and powerful motivator.

For example, a common first answer to "What's Your Why" is money. Almost everybody wants to make more money. There are millions of ways for a person to make more money, both inside and outside the context of their current job or "lot in life." So why do so many fall short of their financial goals? Why do perfectly capable people settle for less? I believe it is because money is overrated in its power to *motivate and change behavior*.

Here's a hypothetical Why scenario, where the Why is money:

Why money? I want to live in a big house.

Why? I grew up in a very small house.

Why? My dad was a laborer, and we had to watch our money pretty close. I had two brothers and we all had to share one bedroom. It was great when we were little, but it got really old later on.

Why? I didn't have any privacy, and my older brothers were always picking on me. I couldn't get away from them. I promised myself that when I grew up, I'd live in a big house.

Why? I now have three boys. I want each of my kids to have his own room, because I don't ever want my youngest to feel like I used to.

Now we are getting somewhere. **Depth** is a key to understanding The Why. You must keep asking until you reach a depth sufficient to motivate and effect changes in behavior. The Why, in this case, isn't money per se; it is a whole set of powerful childhood memories that are now tied directly to the love and concern of this father for his children, perhaps specifically his youngest son.

This father is passionate. He's willing to invest time and effort to honor and realize his vision of how his sons will grow up. For him, the value is priceless, the vision powerful. At this point in his life, it's his treasure. A person's Why is their treasure — and where the treasure is, the heart is. At least, that is where it should be. But more on that later.

Everyone's Why is different. There are common themes, such as success and family — but how The Why manifests itself in a person is uniquely theirs. Normally, it is the single most critical factor that motivates an individual, drives job performance, job satisfaction, and employee loyalty and retention.

Because of its importance in influencing actions, understanding The Why will allow you to know your people better, grow closer to them, and lead them more effectively. It will motivate them and enable them to perform with passion. It also puts you in a position to help each of them lead the life they were destined to lead — a life of significance.

There's also a correlation between The Why and profitability. A friend of mine puts it quite simply: "Happy employees create happy customers, and happy customers buy more stuff."

The amazing thing I have learned is that the majority of leaders, managers, and business owners don't know about, understand, embrace, or leverage The Why. Perhaps they haven't given it enough thought. Maybe they find it too personal. I think it's because many of them don't understand their own Why.

Leaders lead by example. To appreciate someone else's Why, you must first understand your own. Consequently, it's time for you to answer the same question I routinely ask my staff: What's Your Why?

But I don't ask without a little coaching! I have found that one of the easiest ways to help someone discover their Why is with three simple, but absolutely powerful self-analysis questions — I call them the "Big Three." Write down your answers.

What do you think about?

How do you spend your time?

How do you spend your money?

The things we continually think about, spend our time on and spend our money on are, by default, our treasure. These questions, if answered honestly, will reveal where your treasure is, or perhaps what you are making your treasure — whether you like the answers or not. These questions not only help people identify their Why, they also provide a caution when thoughts, actions, and resources drift toward something other than their professed treasure. As an example, it's common for someone to want family to be their Why. However, it's also common that the same people can't prove it when they answer the Big Three. Consequently, the answers to these questions can be a big wake-up call. If you find that there's a real gap between the Why of your heart and the Why of your actions, don't despair. The real value is in the journey to recognize and then actively work on closing that gap.

Whys can be of varying time horizons and are rooted in circumstances, purpose, or both. A Why rooted in circumstance could be a financial tragedy that has created the need to invest an extraordinary amount of time, thought, and money to recover from. In this case, perhaps in a year or two, the tragedy will have passed, giving way to a different Why. The individual could now be free to return to a Why rooted in purpose, such as becoming an artist, or retiring at a certain age to work with abused children.

Answering the Big Three may or may not leave you concerned about your Why. Now let's dig deeper by answering the following questions:

With whom is the most important relationship in your life?

Why?

What is the most important thing in your life?

Why?

What brings you joy?

Why?

What are you passionate about?

Why?

What is your biggest fear?

Why?

What circumstances do you want to avoid in your life?

Why?

If you had a second chance to live your life, what would you "keep" and what would you "change" from the first go-round?

Why?

If you knew you could not fail, what would you be doing?

Why?

As you try to answer the questions, don't accept your first answer at face value. Challenge yourself. There's almost always more to it. Remember that in the earlier example, it took several Whys to get to the real answer.

Are you challenged by the questions? If not, hold your right hand out, palm up. Then place your left index and middle fingers on your right wrist. Check for a pulse. If there is no pulse, stop reading and dial 911. In the event you do detect a pulse, try rereading the questions. Your ability to answer honestly is of the utmost importance. If you aren't aware of the nature and the power of the critical motivating factors in your own life, it will be very challenging to discover and embrace them in others.

Section 3:
What is your Why-Q?

If you can't have empathy and have effective relationships, then no matter how smart you are, you are not going to get very far.

- Daniel Goleman, bestselling author of Emotional Intelligence

Old-economy companies offered longevity and stability to employees in exchange for acquiescence to bureaucracy and a company-focused culture. Put in your time, do a good job, and, in return, the company had a place for you until retirement. Today, longevity and stability for employees are not a part of corporate America's value proposition. In the new economy, there is little loyalty on either side of the paycheck. Companies oblivious to this are destined to mediocrity at best; failure at worst.

As a leader, you have individuals under your direction and care. Some are underperforming and are capable of better work. Others excel, and losing them would be costly. Another group is average and yearning to be noticed, appreciated and inspired. Some will quit and leave; others will quit and stay. How do you effectively manage so many variables?

The Why is a common denominator. No matter where an individual stands developmentally, they have a Why. If you answered the questions in the previous section honestly, you arrived at something both very personal and very powerful in your life. Something you are emotional about, passionate about, and are prepared to make sacrifices for. Guess what? Each of us, including each one of the people you lead, has something equally personal and powerful in their lives. You must learn what it is, **even if that means helping them learn it for themselves.**

The Why demands empathy from a leader; an earnest attempt to place yourself in "another person's shoes." Understanding The Why demonstrates empathy; it communicates "what is important to you is also important to me." It allows you to identify key motivators and harness those motivators to maximize success. Even in today's corporate culture, it's possible to increase the commitment and loyalty of employees. In each case, everyone wins if you discover, acknowledge, and nurture The Why.

Intelligence has traditionally been measured in terms of IQ. I call the ability to understand The Why of your employees your "Why-Q." If you are like most leaders, your Why-Q could stand to improve a few points. A recent conversation I had with an individual revealed the following about her employer's Why-Q:

"I've been here almost three years and I can guarantee not one of the managers has a clue about me personally. If they did, they would be a lot better bosses, and I have no doubt from talking to my colleagues that I'm not alone. They are so concerned about other things I have to believe they aren't really concerned about me."

Ouch. Would any of your reports say this about you? How many of them have you really gotten to know?

To begin developing your Why-Q, complete the following exercise by answering each question for the people that report directly to you. We've left room to write in your answers.

Name of direct report:

What's their Why?

In what way does their current role address his/her Why?

Why did they join your company?

Why do they stay at your company?

Why would they leave your company to do something else?

Where would they go?

What would they do?

Name of direct report:

What's their Why?

In what way does their current role address his/her Why?

Why did they join your company?

Why do they stay at your company?

Why would they leave your company to do something else?

Where would they go?

What would they do?

Name of direct report:

What's their Why?

In what way does their current role address his/her Why?

Why did they join your company?

Why do they stay at your company?

Why would they leave your company to do something else?

Where would they go?

What would they do?

Name of direct report:

What's their Why?

In what way does their current role address his/her Why?

Why did they join your company?

Why do they stay at your company?

Why would they leave your company to do something else?

Where would they go?

What would they do?

Name of direct report:

What's their Why?

In what way does their current role address his/her Why?

Why did they join your company?

Why do they stay at your company?

Why would they leave your company to do something else?

Where would they go?

What would they do?

So how did you do? Does your Why-Q need improvement? If you are like most leaders, the answer is an emphatic "yes!" And remember, in today's economy where quality people are a valuable, fickle, and increasingly scarce resource, understanding their Why can be the leverage you need to both motivate and retain them.

Understanding The Why
Part 1 Summary

You have a treasure. It may take some digging, but it's there.

Where your treasure is, there your heart will be. Answering the right questions with brutal honesty will provide you insight about that treasure.

Your treasure should lead you to your Why — the thing that most powerfully motivates you, influencing your thoughts, planning and actions.

Everyone else also has a treasure — a Why. Empathy is required to understand and appreciate it. Leaders who demonstrate a high Why-Q will get significantly better performance from those they lead.

Part 2
Uncovering The Why

Section 1:
Find Your Power Place

---

*Power is of two kinds. One is obtained by the fear of punishment
and the other by acts of love. Power based on love is a thousand
times more effective and permanent than the one derived from
fear of punishment.*

- Gandhi

Power. It can create and destroy. It can be used for both great benefit and great harm. Its cousins include authority, clout, and control. Webster's defines power as *"one having great authority or influence."* Wow.

Power conjures up all kinds of images. How does your mind react to the mere mention of the following people?

Abraham Lincoln

Your dad

Mother Teresa

Oprah Winfrey

Saddam Hussein

Your best boss ever

Hitler

Bill Gates

Your favorite teacher

Jesus

Your worst boss ever

We all probably agree that each individual listed is (or was) powerful. However, we probably disagree somewhat on our perceptions of those individuals. As a leader (and therefore, someone with power), you are subject to the differing perceptions of those you lead.

In many organizations, the boss sits in the boss's office, and seeing the boss means going to the boss's office…heading upstairs…being "called on the carpet." Very autocratic, very top-down. Excellence today demands something different. It's now a two-way street. Power is distributed differently.

A current marketing buzzword is "interactive." We have interactive TV, interactive games, and interactive appliances. For something to be interactive, an exchange (involving you) must take place. This exchange can sometimes be excruciatingly painful — ever try to program a VCR? Successful interactive products have a very effective user interface — the buttons, levers, or clicks that you use to make it work. Designers and engineers give utmost attention to the user interface. After all, if you can't make the thing work, you either a) won't buy it; or b) won't use it.

Leading people is no different. Your relationship must be interactive, and utmost attention must be given to the user interface. As a leader, you must continually work on your "user interface." It will ultimately determine if your people will "buy (believe) you" or "use (follow) you."

I think that Jesus had the ultimate user interface. He did two key things to influence the hearts and minds of people. First, he spent virtually all his time among them. He didn't sit in some corner office on the top floor of the Jewish temple, waiting for people to be brought to him. He was always moving from place to place, hanging out with the twelve disciples, and enjoying the hospitality of those who would receive him. In Luke 9:58, he remarks, "the Son of Man has no place to lay his head." Jesus knew that it was important to physically *be* with the people he wanted to influence.

Secondly, he knew it was important to meet people with compassion and empathy, regardless of their current stage in life. He gave hope and encouragement to all. He didn't discount them, condescendingly looking down on their sins and shortcomings. How did people respond to Jesus? They changed.

As managers and leaders, what can we learn from that? The lesson is that your power place is with your employees, meeting them "where they are." Get out there among them. Resist the temptation to focus on shortcomings and what they *aren't*. Demonstrate compassion and empathy, give hope, and encourage them.

When is the last time you dropped by and spent time in somebody's cube who is not a "direct report" of yours?

My business partner, Garth Young, makes it a point to take all of our employees to lunch — one on one — over the course of each year (his treat). A small percentage, if any, of the conversation is about work. It's relaxed, the atmosphere encourages sharing, and it communicates to our people that he cares.

The *power place principle* certainly has applications in parenting. I have two teenagers. Although it took me some time to figure it out, I realized that I have better interactions them when we are engaged in an activity that we both enjoy. *Shared activities are power places.* Golf, euchre, scrapbooking, working out, softball, fantasy football, or social events are all great examples of opportunities to spend time with your people in a setting that will help you develop interactive relationships.

Many still try to manage from afar, but that's not where it's at in the twenty-first century workplace. Finding a power place with each of your people is paramount to increasing your Why-Q.

Do not underestimate the influence of a power place. Have you ever stared at a mountain or looked out across the ocean and suddenly felt like a different person? Have you ever noticed both at home and at work that you tend to gravitate to certain room or area because it just "feels" better? A power place feels comfortable and safe. There is no better environment for putting away the formalities of the workplace, allowing you to really communicate and share with someone. If done properly, the power place helps to motivate, inspire, and create shared empathy as well as build loyalty — all priceless treasures, indeed.

Section 2:
Getting to the Heart of the Matter

You must capture and keep the heart of the original and supremely able man before his brain can do its best.

- Andrew Carnegie

I attended Indiana University in the early '80s. One of the highlights of my college experience was witnessing the men's basketball team win the 1981 NCAA Championship. Indiana Coach Bobby Knight said something during that era that stuck with me. He said, "Sometimes, I want these kids to be great more than *they* want to be great." More than twenty years later, I understand exactly how the coach was feeling when he said that.

Uncovering The Why requires an investment of the heart — your heart. It is a process that will happen in increments. It also takes time, which is a valuable resource.

It's very easy to become lost in the business of doing business. It happens to all of us. The time we intend to spend getting to know our people better gets put off for a few hours and then for a few days. Days then turn into months, and months turn into years. We apathetically default to a mode in which we aren't close to our people, and they aren't close to us. We experience turnover, and wonder why. Or even worse, we expect it, and are numb to its occurrence.

Who wants to be part of an organization like that? Nobody does, certainly not the people who work there.

We often do these things because we are more concerned with our own plans than the plans of those we lead. We reduce the equation to asking them if they like their job, and they nod yes. We pay them market value, based on our own biases and rationalizations. Then, we forget **the person** working for us, and go back to business as usual.

Understanding conceptually that your power place is among your people, meeting them where they are is a great start. Now there is work to be done.

Think of something special that you truly love to do. Something that, for you, is more than an activity — it's an event. You appreciate the details and savor the nuances. Thoughts of a baseball game bring the warmth of the sun on a summer day; vendors selling hot dogs, peanuts, and beer; the smell of popcorn, the crack of the bat as it hits the ball.

I simply love going to the Indiana State Fair. Each summer, I can hardly wait for it to arrive. I love the lights on the midway after dark; the smell of elephant ears; the taste of milkshakes, corn on the cob, turkey legs, and lemon shake-ups; going into the animal barns, marveling at the draft horses and watching my youngest daughter pet the baby pigs. It's rich. The question is, can you transfer that kind of passion to engaging with your employees?

You can go to the movies, but not really smell the popcorn. You can stand at the edge of the ocean, but not really feel the sand and the waves on your feet. You can engage in these activities and still miss the point. Half-hearted and insincere attempts to uncover The Why won't work. You've got to want them to be great, sometimes even more than *they* want to be great.

Who does Allan most want to be like? What drives Keith to succeed? Where does Beth want to be in five years? What is Anna's timetable to accomplish her life's goal? Why does Sara work so hard? To **obtain** an understanding of these things, you must **seek** an understanding of these things.

As I mentioned earlier, uncovering The Why requires an investment of the heart. Your power place is where your people feel comfortable sharing with you who they really are. This is a critical step to truly harnessing the passion inside them. It also means rolling up your sleeves and getting your hands dirty.

The concept of the "burning have-to" will reveal clues to The Why of an employee. What's the burning have-to? My father had a one of the best examples that I can think of.

Dad graduated from high school in 1960 at age seventeen. He enrolled and started at the local college, but soon chose to leave and find a job. At nineteen, he found himself married and expecting a child. My mom and I became his burning have-to. Over the next couple of years, he held several different jobs before landing on the assembly line at the Whirlpool Corporation plant in Evansville, Indiana, roughly an hour's drive from our home. It started out rough. On his first day, the foreman assigned him to a task on an assembly line that was very involved, with lots of pieces. Not a job for a "newbie." The first thing the other guys on the line tried to do was "break" him and get him to quit. The men proceeded to set the line speed a little fast, so that the pieces came at him faster than normal. Each time Dad missed a piece, the line was stopped and the other men gave him a hard time. Within the first hour his hands were bleeding, as he hadn't developed the calluses on his hands that were necessary to do that particular job for any length of time. However, Dad kept going, and by noon, it must have become clear that he wasn't going to quit. The foreman intervened and moved him to a more appropriate job for a new employee on his first day.

My dad's burning have-to of a wife and new baby kept him going as he made the hour commute each way to work in the factory. In time, he switched to night shift and enrolled once again at the local college. He worked all night, drove home, took a shower, and then attended his classes for the day. He slept in the afternoon and early evening, before rising to do it all again.

I still remember attending his graduation in 1969. I was eight years old. It was customary for immediate family members to stand as the graduate received their diploma. When Dad's name was read, my grandma nudged me and said "Stand up, that's your dad." His burning have-to drove him passionately to accomplish his goals. My dad has gone on to become a successful educator and businessman.

There are people in your company who have a burning have-to, just like my dad.

A good friend of mine has a great question that he asks prospective employees as part of his interview process to get at their Why. He instructs them to imagine that they own a stand that sells pizza by the slice. They are able to buy pizza slices for $1 each, and then sell them for $2 each. He also tells them that, magically, there will always be someone standing there asking to buy a piece of pizza, twenty-four hours a day, seven days a week. As soon as one customer goes, another appears, ready to purchase. He then poses two questions. The first is: "How many hours a day are you going to be open for business?" The second question is simply, "Why?" When you ask questions like this, you begin to gain valuable insight to what motivates a person and the reasons for it. If there's a burning have-to, it should surface. Again, don't accept the superficial. Depth is the key.

Whatever you do, find a way to get to the heart of the matter. Sometimes in the process, you discover a fatal flaw that cannot be corrected. The Why then allows you to avoid or eliminate a problem before it does more damage, as this true story from one of my clients illustrates.

Alcoholic Ambition

A new executive was hired to reform a lagging division of a Fortune 500 company. One of his first tasks was to interview all key people and determine who the top performers were. Almost immediately, he encountered Simon, a mid-level manager who enthusiastically expressed his desire to move up the company ladder, willing to do whatever it took.

Simon was smart, articulate and — from all appearances to the new manager — seemed up to the challenge. His instincts told him there must be some reason Simon's enthusiasm hadn't already resulted in promotion, but the previous manager wasn't a strong leader and he surmised that must have contributed to Simon's lack of progression.

Over time, a pattern emerged: Simon would be given more responsibility and he would perform well for a time, only to then fail for inexplicable reasons. He would be late to work, he would take critical days off, his attention to detail was lacking. Luckily, the new manager had begun to develop strong relationships with other employees by utilizing power places. In doing so, he quickly learned valuable information from others who had known Simon for years. Unfortunately, Simon was an alcoholic. Upon confrontation, Simon was surprisingly open about his alcohol problem. He had never been confronted about it before and apparently thought he could get away with it. The new manager did his best to get Simon help but unfortunately, the alcohol problem was never solved and he was eventually let go. The manager learned a valuable lesson. Appearances can be deceiving. Depth is the key. Sometimes potential, or potential disaster, lies underneath.

Section 3:

Diamonds in the Rough

You are, at this moment, standing, right in the middle of your own "acres of diamonds."

- Earl Nightingale, Chairman of Nightengale-Conant

In their raw form, diamonds are black, look like coal, and don't at all resemble the dazzling gems they will become. If you or I were in a diamond mine but didn't know it, we would look around and just see rocks. Our untrained eyes would see nothing of value. Guess what? Your business is a lot like a diamond mine. Some of your people, no doubt, just look like lumps of coal to you.

In the Disney movie, *Aladdin,* the magic lamp lies deep inside the mysterious Cave of Wonders. During the early scenes, the evil Jafar attempts to get the lamp by sending Gazeem, a common thief, into the cave. As soon as he enters, however, the cave senses an intruder and swallows Gazeem alive. A booming voice announces *"Only one may enter, one whose worth lies deep within. Seek thee out the Diamond in the Rough."*

Kirk Abraham came to my company in the summer of 2000. He had spent five years in the U.S. Marine Corps and another five years as a production supervisor at Ford Motor Company. Smart, funny and ambitious, Kirk was convinced there was something in his future beyond the factory floor. However, he had no sales experience and was very rough around the edges.

We took a chance, hired him, and soon learned that Kirk felt he had lots to prove; to others, and to himself. Although extremely bright, he lacked confidence due to a history of being overlooked in favor of more refined intellectual types. He was the class clown, so he often wasn't taken seriously. To many, Kirk was a lump of coal.

As we sought to understand him, we got a handle on Kirk's Why. He came to us thirsting to prove to himself, his family and the world that he was just as talented and capable as the MBAs and marine guys who used to reside above him on the food chain.

Kirk displayed a strong work ethic and a willingness to learn. He listened and honed his craft every day. Oh, he made mistakes, but he always meant well, and it was hard to stay mad at him. As time progressed, the lump of coal began to look like a diamond.

He continuously set goals for himself, and each year his production increased. He watched training videos, read books, listened to tapes in his car, and interviewed some of the giants in our business. It has paid off handsomely for both Kirk and our company. In each of the past two years, he has been our top-producing account executive, outperforming all others in a very competitive environment full of talented salespeople. Although Kirk is still growing, now, even an untrained eye sees a diamond.

No position in an organization is exempt from this phenomenon. Understanding and uncovering The Why allows you to help people shine. As they shine, so do you. You must develop an "Eye for The Why." Every person in your organization has untapped potential, make it your mission to find it.

There are people like Kirk in your company right now. When you look around in the diamond mine that is your business, what do you see? Do you see untold riches and beauty, or just rocks? The diamonds are there. Can you unleash their power?

Uncovering The Why
Part 2 Summary

The balance of power has shifted. The employer-employee relationship is far more collaborative than it once was.

As a leader, you must continually work on your user interface.

Your power place is among your people, meeting them where *they* are, not where you expect them to be.

A power place is a physical place or activity where formality is not required and sharing can take place.

You must make an investment of the heart to uncover The Why.

There are diamonds all over your company, but some of them look like lumps of coal right now.

Part 3
Unleashing The Why

Section 1:
Sharing The Why

If we treasure our own experience and regard it as real, we must also treasure other people's experience.

- John C. Polanyi, Nobel Laureate

Sharing The Why is critical to unleashing the power inside your people. **You've got to make their Why your Why.** Sharing The Why creates a Why culture, the effect of which transcends personal, one-on-one meetings and impacts both organizational morale and the bottom line. When this synergy takes place, buried treasure begins to surface.

Tammi Ramsey is a very special person at my company. An amateur winemaker who has produced award-winning wines on both a local and national level, Tammi's dream is to live and own a vineyard in California. My partners and I understand this. Tammi's goal is our goal. In 2004, Tammi took a huge step toward her dream by purchasing eighty-seven acres of land in California. Contractors soon were on site, constructing a building to house equipment she would purchase someday. As her dream was coming true, life threw her a curve ball.

Tammi became ill and was diagnosed with thyroid cancer. Although the prognosis was promising, she faced weeks of radiation therapy and all the related challenges that come with it. She missed a great deal of work. Her billable projects disappeared. Although Tammi is compensated 100 percent on commission, we continued to support her financially, with no prospects for a return on our investment. It was the right thing to do.

When Tammi came back to work, she shared with us how overwhelmed she was by the commitment of our company and our employees to her during her illness and recovery. At the end of 2005, Tammi moved to California to pursue her dream.

Why does Tammi come back after cancer and chemotherapy to work for us? Why didn't she just take that life-changing event as her cue to get her tail to California — pronto? Because we shared her Why. It created a powerful bond.

Earlier, I shared the story of my dad and his burning have-to. The same foreman who was involved in the assembly line prank on my dad's first day turned out to be a "Why guy."

As time went on, that foreman watched my dad work. He must have seen something in him that he liked, because he began spending more time with my dad. He began to teach my dad different jobs, and eventually taught him all forty-four jobs that comprised that particular assembly line. He then pulled my dad off of his specific job on the line and made him a "floater." As a floater, his job was to be available and ready to jump in at any time, for any job on the line, when necessary. If someone called in sick, quit, was transferred, needed a bathroom break, or was injured, my dad stepped in and did whatever job was required to keep the line running.

The foreman also knew that my dad was enrolled in college. The nature of his job provided Dad with time each shift where he was between assignments. The foreman told him that he should bring his books so he could study during his down time. Dad took advantage of this, and was able to work and study at the same time.

Why did the foreman do that? I think it was because, although he may not have realized it, he understood my dad's Why. Perhaps he saw a bit of himself in my dad, and he wanted my dad to make it out of the factory. Perhaps he wished that someone would have helped him get out of the factory years ago. We'll never know for sure, but that foreman played a part in my dad's future, and consequently mine. When you help someone realize their Why, you just don't know how much impact you can have. You can literally change the course of generations.

Morgan Stanley once had a great commercial in which a man is speaking at a groundbreaking ceremony. He goes on and on, praising everyone and expressing heartfelt gratitude to all who helped make the day possible. As he speaks, the camera cuts to the two business owners, who are both holding shovels, eagerly waiting to perform the ceremonial dig. One says to the other, "Bob, how long are you going to let your Morgan Stanley guy go on?" It was comical. The Morgan Stanley advisor understood the motivation of the business owner to grow and build his business. He made The Why of that business owner *his own* Why as well. When the dream became reality, he appeared more excited than his client.

The key to authentic engagement with your employees is sharing their Why. It allows you to help them reach their potential, achieve their dreams and change their lives. Common understanding leads to common bond. It's amazing what can happen when you put it all together.

Section 2:
Motivating with The Why

Motivation is the art of getting people to do what you want them to do because they want to do it.
- Dwight D. Eisenhower, thirty-fourth president of the United States

Much has been written about motivation over the years, and much more will be written in the future. In *Think and Grow Rich,* Napoleon Hill referred to motivation as "that state of mind known as burning desire," and declared it "the starting point of all achievement." The factors that motivate us are complex and often work in strange combinations that are hard to understand.

Motivating with The Why is an art; a craft that must be honed by ***doing***. It is not a science. There is no formula, and one size does not fit all. You must jump in, get your hands dirty, and figure it out for each person you lead. In larger organizations, the ability to connect and invest may be limited to your direct reports. You must be the model, the example your direct reports follow in dealing with the people entrusted to them.

The key to motivating effectively with The Why is accumulated personal equity. You must have enough equity and trust with your people to "go there."

The Why is very personal and powerful, and cannot be taken lightly or used indiscriminately. You must develop a "feel" for each person you manage to know how best to motivate them with their Why.

If an employee's Why is affirmation, motivate with frequent praise and recognition. If it's challenge, motivate by assigning a difficult project. Some may respond best to an appeal or gentle nudge: "You and I both know you're better than this…" Others may require a more direct approach: "You're letting your family down…." Candor is essential. Sometimes, velvet gloves work best; other times it may take a sledgehammer. Care enough to tell them the truth. As the book of Proverbs says, "Wounds from a friend can be trusted."

Use power places to interact and talk about the things that matter most. Look for ways to leverage these things to inspire and fuel performance. It's critical to make this link. Don't settle for the superficial. What is it that they really seek? To make a parent proud? To prove a parent wrong? To impress an ex-spouse? To overcome childhood adversity? To erase lingering self-doubt?

Reconnect your people to their Why on a regular basis. Call it a reality check, call it whatever you like, but understand that it's critical. The art as a leader is to understand the motivators, understand whether they are rooted in positive or negative experiences, and leverage them for good.

Outside forces are always attempting to steer us off course. Therefore, we must monitor ourselves like a ship's captain monitors an ocean voyage. The Why serves as a compass, providing direction and reminding us of our *raison d'etre*.

One of the interesting things about The Why is how easily it can become lost or misplaced. People sometimes lose motivation or lose focus. They become confused when other factors masquerade as motivators. Sometimes it's laziness, sometimes it's denial, sometimes it's an innocent lack of focus. This is where the art of motivating with The Why really comes into play.

Here are real-life examples from of my clients, in their own words, illustrating what happens when you use The Why to motivate and what happens when you don't.

"I was trying to hire a top performer who had offers from several other firms and I was offering less money. I understood that this candidate knew he had a great deal of potential and would succeed at whatever career path he set for himself. I spent some time getting to know this person well and determined his Why. My goal was to help him see how I could get him to realize it.

"He wanted to be a senior executive of a Fortune 500 company so I asked him how he saw himself getting there. He was only able to articulate one path that would reach this goal. I then laid out the paths of five senior executives at our company, which were all different, and I specifically explained the rationale for the steps each had taken to reach their goals.

"I then offered suggestions on how he could accelerate the process of becoming a senior executive. At this point, I could have offered him less money and he still would have accepted the job because I was able to confidently answer his Why and hire him as a senior manager.

"One year after I hired him, he was promoted and after two years, completed his MBA from Northwestern, the nation's top graduate business school. More importantly, he became an executive after only two years with the organization. Word got around, and I now have a strong supply of top people who want to join my organization. Even if he eventually leaves, my company, my career, and his career are better off."

Another real-life example from one of my clients, John Oblazney:

"Early in my career, I hired a gentleman in his early thirties who I felt had a lot of potential, with strengths that offset some of my weaknesses. I also knew that integral to his Why was to have my job someday. I wanted someone preferably stronger than myself, so I promised him that he would be given my job in approximately two years. I knew that in two years, my MBA would be finished, and I would be ready to move up the ladder.

"After only six months, I asked him if he felt prepared for my position. He gave me a strange look like I was kidding, or perhaps nuts. (The move from his position to mine was great and would be more than a 100% increase in his salary from what he was making at his former employer.) I wasn't kidding, and I wasn't nuts. Immediately after hiring him, I began to teach him the nuances of the business and began to give him additional responsibility and comprehensive exposure to the organization.

"Because of this exposure, my organization was able to recognize his strong analytical skills and leadership abilities. Within a year of his employment, I was able to present him to the organization as a future replacement for me. The response was mixed, so I increased his job scope and offered him more mentoring. He performed as expected and, within six months, I posed the question to my organization again. The same people who had said no six months previously gave him an emphatic yes.

"Due to a lack of available growth opportunities, it now looked like that for my protégé to take my place, I would have to move on to another company instead of up my own company's ladder. I was no longer working for the kind of manager who understood my Why, or anyone else's for that matter. My boss moved on and was replaced with a mediocre player who got the job based on the reputation that

comes with an Ivy League education. I asked him what my current opportunities were in the company, and he said that he did not see himself going anywhere in the near future and that I should sit tight for a couple of years and wait to see what opens up.

"My next opportunity was to be his successor so I asked him what his career plans were and he stated it 'wasn't up to him.' He was so casual about it all that I cringed inside. Two weeks after I finished my MBA, I asked again about opportunities in the company and he stated that I was one of the most highly rated managers in the company and something should open up sometime in the future, but he was not sure what or when. The next day, I resigned to go work for a top performer like my previous boss had been. I subsequently learned that this individual had been given three things he must do to succeed in his role as CFO. One of those three things was to keep me as an employee. Had he understood The Why and been someone who cared about my Why, he might have succeeded. He didn't and he failed. Miserably.

"The young man I had hired to replace me, did indeed replace me and was very grateful for everything. He said he had never met anyone like me before. I smiled and apologized because I was five days past my two-year promise. He asked how could he ever repay me. I responded, 'Do the same for somebody you lead. Uncover their Why and make it happen.'

"Three months after I left, the transition was seamless and he was doing well. My protégé had the job and all the money he wanted. He was comfortable and happy. However, I needed to build a strong team at my new company and eliminate deadweight. I went to him and asked him to work for me again, and help develop a strong team. I shared my vision and told him I was excited about the possibility of him joining our group. The position I offered was a reduction in title and position. His wife thought he was nuts, considering he had just gotten the job *he had coveted for such a long time. But because he believed in me and my ability to help him realize his Why, he quit his job and came to work for me again.*

"We proceeded to build one of the greatest teams in our company, moved the organization to levels it had never achieved, and set a new bar for others to strive. After two years with him, I was promoted and moved on. Needless to say, he replaced me again and is now in an executive position making four times what he was the day we first met less than seven years ago."

So there you have it, the power of The Why in action. It should motivate you and it should sober you. The organizations that allowed The Why to grow prospered; those that didn't suffered.

What struck me most was the vision these managers exhibited. John understood that to reach his ultimate goal — running a Fortune 500 company — it is critical to build a network of people who understand The Why. In order to leave behind a trail of success, he selflessly improved every person he led; even if it meant losing them to better opportunities with another company. John Oblazney has become known as someone who makes the people around him better, and that is the type of person who achieves their Why, no matter what it is.

These examples are not unique. There are people like these in your organization right now. The Why is a powerful motivating force. More importantly, by motivating with The Why and using this power to uncover the diamonds, you truly unleash the full potential of those you lead.

Section 3:
Mentoring with The Why

My values and beliefs were imparted to me by loving parents,
committed teachers, demanding mentors and wise elders.

- Jesse Helms, five-term United States senator

I describe the way we lead at my company as "walking beside our employees, rather than standing over them." It's a powerful metaphor that conveys, in my view, the essence of mentoring. I define mentoring as a relationship characterized by shared empathy for and commitment to a person and their success.

Mentoring involves investing, teaching and challenging. Mentoring builds people up, and sometimes requires picking people up. It expects the best, yet recognizes that we will at times fall short of expectations. Mentoring with The Why is the last piece to the puzzle that unlocks the power hidden inside your people. An environment in which an individual's Why is addressed as business needs are met creates a powerful synergy which drives higher levels of performance. Everybody wins.

Once you find what someone is passionate about, that passion can be contagious and intoxicating. Author Donald Miller never liked jazz music. But one night on the streets of Portland he encountered a man playing the saxophone. Miller stopped. He stood there for fifteen minutes watching, and the musician never opened his eyes. After that, Donald Miller liked jazz music.

Seeing somebody love something is sometimes necessary before you can love it yourself. It is as if they are showing you the way.

People in touch with The Why exude passion. When they transfer it to the work, it's as if they are showing others in the organization the way. The same people gravitate toward the passion and the activity, even if they are not initially interested.

What would change by getting someone to transfer their passion to reducing customer complaints, improving scrap loss, or increasing the number of on-time deliveries? Are you willing to consider that all those things just might get measurably better? Are you also willing to consider that the people involved in making this happen will thrive in the process?

It can happen, and it starts with understanding the keys to mentoring. They are

Model the behavior
Equity with the people
Nobody is excluded
Time investment
Open and honest communication
Repetition and accountability

Model the behavior:

It all starts at the top. Whether you lead an entire company or a small department, you must model the appropriate behavior. All eyes are on you, regardless of your willingness to acknowledge it. If you expect your direct reports to be effective mentors, you must be the best possible example. They will be motivated by it.

Equity with the people:

The formula is:

Equity = Connection + Investment + Empathy

Connection: Nothing happens unless a connection is made. Connections happen best in the absence of formality. Resist any impulse to make the process overly formalized. Set aside the end game initially. Focus on the person first, outcomes second. Find common ground. Let them see who you are, and they'll start to show you who they are. Be transparent, and you will receive transparency in return.

Investment: Once the connection is made, it's important to make investments in the relationship. You've heard the saying, "the best way to make a friend is to be a friend." The same applies here. In today's 24/7 world, people's most important resource is time. It's finite and it's unrecoverable. When you devote time to someone, you are communicating that you care in a powerful way. When you spend some of that time helping someone find their treasure, you build equity.

Empathy: Remember, you can't reach someone until you understand them. You can't understand them until you *seek* to understand them. Empathy is a powerful emotion. It is through showing sincere interest in the things that are most important to your people that you will learn their dreams and identify the most powerful motivating factors in their life. Empathy and time are your two most powerful tools for building equity.

People join companies, but they leave managers. I have very candid conversations daily with individuals who are looking to leave their employer. A common theme is problems with their manager.

It is rare, however, that I am contacted by someone looking for a new job who says, "I love my boss." Conversely, it's hard for me (or anyone, for that matter) to recruit a candidate who says, "I have a great boss who's done a wonderful job of helping me meet my personal and professional goals." How many people leave a boss like that? As a leader, you must be an advocate for employee growth, for their Why. In this regard, The Why often acts as a magnet for retention.

Nobody is excluded:

It's important that a mentoring culture be an inclusive culture. Otherwise, there is a good chance that your employee population will segregate into the "haves" and the "have-nots." Avoiding this is easier said than done, and requires striking a balance between legislating mentoring relationships and allowing them to evolve.

Mentoring relationships originate in many ways. They develop informally based on personality, proximity, or other common attributes between individuals. There are times when a manager or leader "picks" an individual to mentor based on an instinct her or she has — they "see something" and want to take a personal role in searching it or developing it. Some individuals aggressively seek a mentor for themselves. There are, however, many people within companies who don't fall into these categories. Herein lies a huge, untapped opportunity. Think for a moment of the people in your organization. How many of them have a mentor? Who is taking a personal interest in each of them? What would happen to their performance if you started walking beside them, and convinced them that the thing most important to them was also very important to you? The inclusiveness principle is absolutely critical.

Time:

Some will argue that they don't have the time or the energy to mentor. Some will bemoan the "cost." The time and energy invested in the mentoring relationship certainly has a bottom-line impact, and it should be positive. That time and energy is going to be invested somewhere; how about investing it where the return is arguably the highest? An effective mentoring program will actually save management time, benefiting mentors, those being mentored, and the organization as a whole. It will make you money.

Open and honest communication:

Everything works better in an environment of open and honest communication. People want to hear the truth, even if it's painful. As you spend time making investments in the relationship, the exchange of information becomes increasingly real. Opportunities to offer insight and guidance will appear. Take advantage of those opportunities. Practice the art of asking good questions. Ask questions that require your people to synthesize information, evaluate options and suggest the best course of action.

Allow them to make decisions. Acknowledge and praise "good calls." When mistakes are made, don't get mad. Start by asking, "What did you learn?," or "What would you do differently next time?" Then, provide opportunities for them to apply what they have learned. The return on these investments will be enormous to you, your people, and your organization.

Repetition and accountability:

Repetition: There are two messages that must be delivered regularly. The first is macro-level repetition of the basic Why concept. It must be repeated and reinforced frequently. Some in the organization will no doubt resist. Their will be those who simply don't believe it. There will be others who don't respect its power. Perhaps some must see it work before they will embrace it. Whatever the circumstance, continue to reinforce the Why concept and the reason it makes sense.

The second is micro-level repetition of each individual's Why. Those committed to their Why will occasionally lose sight of it. There are many things vying for their attention. People find themselves climbing a ladder that's suddenly leaning against the wrong wall. The comfort zone is an enemy of the Why. When times get tough, they may try to rationalize their behavior relative to their Why or numb themselves to its importance. Don't let this slide.

Repetition is also important to the element of accountability.

Accountability: This is a touchy subject, and thus must be handled carefully. The first step is to properly educate on the concept of accountability. The "default" perception of most is that accountability is punitive. That is, I am going to "call you out" because you didn't meet your goal, didn't do what you said, etc. It's very important that you repeatedly communicate that punishment is not the objective.

Reinforce that accountability is something that communicates you care about them. This is a tough lesson for some to learn, especially in our current culture, which spends so much time avoiding personal responsibility. You must establish accountability as both healthy and necessary for individuals and the organization to maximize their capabilities.

A person's Why is presumably the most personal, powerful motivator in their life. They have given you a glimpse of their treasure. Your job is to walk alongside them to make sure they find it. Remember that searching for treasure is not easy. Think about it: Treasure hunters are usually hungry, tired, dirty, and frustrated. It's mostly uphill. It requires perseverance, resilience and time.

Zig Ziglar says that to get what you want, you must help enough other people get what they want. What they want is their Why. Their Why, to a certain extent, then becomes one of your Whys.

This communicates "Because you have told me this is of supreme importance to you, I am going to help you get there, even if it means pushing you and stretching you." Accountability is critical to the effectiveness of the mentoring relationship. Although most of us acknowledge the value of being held accountable, we usually don't like it when someone actually does it to us. Appreciating being held accountable is an "acquired taste." The more it happens, the easier it becomes, and the more we appreciate it.

As a leader, a "boss," you can dictate accountability, but the best accountability relationships are those where permission is granted. Once you have agreement that the accountability relationship is about *them*, and exists for the purpose of helping them find their treasure — their Why — you will be granted permission to hold them accountable. The goal is mutual agreement that accountability, if done properly, is a healthy thing which offers significant opportunities for personal and professional growth.

It doesn't have to be adversarial, and if done correctly, rarely will be. Often, holding someone accountable is simply asking a couple of questions, such as "How did it happen?" and "What did you learn from this?" It won't always be this easy. Some people won't get it. Consequently, if you keep having the same conversations with someone, there's a problem and you may have to turn up the heat. It will be your call based on the situation. Once again, we're talking about an art, not a science.

And what about obstacles, you ask? Henry Ford said that obstacles are those frightful things you see when you take your eyes off your goal. Implementing a Why culture is not easy. If it were, more companies would do it. It's hard investing the time, energy, and heart necessary to lead at this level. And it's not all under your control. You'll have to deal with:

Changing Whys: The Why will change over time for some of your people, especially long-term employees and those with a Why rooted in specific accomplishments. If an individual's Why is to put all five kids through college without student loans, what's the encore? This is why it is so important to be continuously mentoring. It gives you the ability to dig deep and head off potential Why problems before they manifest themselves as management problems.

Toxic employees: There will certainly be some. They can poison even the best Why culture. You may experience everything from skepticism to outright sabotage. Some can be won over with success stories or intense mentoring. Others may have to go.

The Unknown Why: You will find that some don't have a clue what their Why is. What a great way to bond with someone. Help them identify their treasure, then go help them find it. Start with the Big Three, and go from there.

Negative or Destructive Whys: Some may know exactly what their Why is — and it isn't good. Some are motivated by the chance to undermine others or make them look bad. Look here for congruence between what they say and what they do. If you uncover negative or harmful intentions, they must change or go.

False Whys: These can take many forms. In some cases, a false Why results from someone not being honest with themselves. Whys which are not of sufficient depth or are very short-term in their timeframe are apt to be false Whys. Another reason you must dig deep.

Resentment of The Why: What happens if you don't like your Why? It's clear, based on your thoughts, words, and actions, but you don't like it. One individual recently shared with me that his Why was to make enough money to care for his aging parents. He also shared with me that he was resentful that this burden fell to him, and not to others in the family. This might be best addressed by digging deep in search of a Why born of purpose, in addition to this particular Why born of circumstance.

Betrayal of The Why: What if people aren't being true to The Why? If there is an inconsistency between word and action, then it's probably not a Why. As a mentor, you must hold them accountable and shine light on the inconsistency. Mentor them to their real Why and hold them to it.

All of these obstacles can be overcome, and when you do, you will unleash the power inside those you lead. You will find treasure. Relationships will be richer. Lives will change. Work will become a mission — a mission of passion, connection, and accomplishment.

Unleashing The Why
Part 3 Summary

Common understanding leads to common bond. You must share The Why.

Motivating with The Why is an art.

People in touch with their Why exude passion. That passion is contagious.

Mentoring is the key to an organization fueled by The Why. As a leader, you must model the behavior and replicate those behaviors in others.

Equity with all of your people is essential. Invest the time necessary to develop it. Everyone must be included in the mentoring process.

Repeating The Why concept and individual Whys is essential. Hold people accountable in a positive manner with open and honest communication.

You will encounter obstacles, and that's where you must hone your craft.

Epilogue
Where Is Your Treasure?

A box without hinges, key, or lid,
yet golden treasure inside is hid.
- J. R. R. Tolkien

Companies spend huge amounts of time, energy, and money looking outside for treasure: improved revenue, profitability, morale, loyalty, and retention, to name a few. They often overlook the power of seeking the treasure *inside.*

The treasure lies in The Why. Your job as a leader is to seek that treasure in your people with the same passion that led explorers to Robinson Crusoe Island for almost 300 years. When you harness the power of The Why, treasure will appear. Diamonds will reveal themselves in surprising places. They may be right below the surface. The treasure of Robinson Crusoe Island was only fifty feet underground. You must know where to dig, and how deep to dig.

Success stories are waiting to unfold all over your company. How many can you bring to reality? Creating a Why culture is the place to start, and it will lead to individual as well as organizational success. You will unleash energy and performance that is contagious, intoxicating and transforming.

Where your treasure is, there your heart will be. Let The Why transform you and those you lead. It will lead to success and significance for both you and them. So put the book down and get to work right now. Grab an employee, find a power place, look them in the eye, and ask:

What's Your Why?

Appendix
Getting Started with The Why
and Recommended Reading

To get started with The Why, follow these steps:

Step 1: Go through the process of discovering your own treasure. Write it out; define it simply and clearly.

Step 2: Allow your treasure to lead you to a definition of your Why.

Step 3: Take an inventory of your people. For how many do you know their Why?

Step 4: Get out of your office. Find power places that you and each of your people feel comfortable with.

Step 5: Connect. Invest. Dig deep. Ask questions. Look for leverage points that are meaningful motivators.

Step 6: Emphasize. Share The Why. Commit it to memory, make note cards, do whatever you must to mentally link individuals to their Why.

Step 7: Leverage The Why to motivate each individual. Look for the underutilized Diamonds in the Rough. Implement a mentoring program applying the **MENTOR** principles to create momentum that will result in higher levels of performance.

Common Management Problems
Solved with The Why:

Problem 1: A key member of my team unexpectedly left, and I'm afraid the upheaval could lead to more turnover.

Answer: Gather your team leaders and discuss The Why of the former team member. How defined was it? What could have been done to keep them? Segue into a discussion of "Where are we with The Why" of other key people. Is anyone else at risk? This is a great opportunity to "wake up" your mentors.

Problem 2: For the last month, my key manager has seemed downbeat and less productive, and I haven't been able to figure it out.

Answer: Changes in work behavior are a red flag; head to a power place and offer help. Use the equity you have accumulated with the individual to diagnose the problem quickly.

Problem 3: I feel like my staff has become complacent.

Answer: How about having a group Why session focusing on the collective success of the group? There's art involved here. Is it a group problem or rooted in specific individuals?

Problem 4: I'm having trouble hiring top performers I'm interviewing, and I don't know why.

Answer: Review your interview strategy and determine to what extent The Why is being utilized in the hiring process. If you don't understand the key motivators that drive a prospective candidate to make career decisions, you probably can't hire them.

Problem 5: I have to move one of my best performers to another position. What if this creates dissent?

Answer: Does the move allow the individual to stay connected to their Why? If not, make sure you have to move them.

Problem 6: A valued employee is ready for his or her next assignment, and I don't have an opportunity at this time.

Answer: Empathy is your best tool. Be sure THEY understand that YOU understand they are getting frustrated. Develop a plan where they can clearly see a career path. If this isn't possible, perhaps you'd be best served helping them find opportunity in another company while they help you find a replacement.

Problem 7: My best manager has lost direction. How do I get him or her back on track with their Why?

Answer: Be ready for multiple meetings and don't try to fix the problem too quickly. Start with the basics; reconnect with their Why and trace the path that allowed it to become "lost." Working through issues like this allows you to build terrific loyalty.

Problem 8: One of my team members is underperforming, not meeting expectations, causing problems, missing work, etc.

Answer: Attempt to diagnose with The Why. Be aware that multiple, random symptoms may be a sign of serious problems. Be on your guard; don't let a bad seed drive away your best performers.

Problem 9: I'm the manager and I'm confused about my Why.

Answer: You are not alone. It's common for managers to get so caught up in the responsibility of managing that they forget about themselves. Start with the basics and make sure you have a mentor that can advise you and hold you accountable. Go back to the Big Three. Dig deep. Ask Why a lot.

Recommended Reading List from Kent

Think and Grow Rich - Napoleon Hill

In my view, the best business book of its kind. A comprehensive, step-by-step guide to making your dreams come true. A valuable resource to share with those you mentor.

The Little Red Book of Selling - Jeff Gitomer

The Little Red Book of Sales Answers - Jeff Gitomer

Whether you're in sales or not, you are always selling — to the boss, to your co-workers, to your kids, you name it. You have to sell importance of The Why to your people to make it work for everyone. Practical advice on how to get maximum results.

Negotiate This! - Herb Cohen

All of life is a negotiation. This book outlines the key concepts that you must be aware of to achieve the results that you desire when dealing with others. Can be a key resource in managing mentor relationships.

Recommended Reading
List from Silouan

The Road Less Traveled - M. Scott Peck

No book better explains what drives and influences modern man. Read this and apply it as you hone your craft with The Why.

The Art of War - Sun Tzu

Written thousands of years ago, it is the foundation of all effective business strategy. Referenced in the boardrooms of Fortune 500 companies and on the battlefields by our military leaders.

The Collected Philokalia - Various Monks

Essays on the emotional and spiritual state of man. Written over a period of hundreds of years by monks who devoted their lives to understanding the condition of their soul. Read this and come to a deeper understanding of fundamental truths that influence all people regardless of their religious affiliations and beliefs.

Notes

Made in the USA
Middletown, DE
17 November 2018